MILLENNIUM MANIA

MILLENNIUM MANIAM

**Fascinating Facts and Quotes
for the Dawn of the 21st Century**

STEPHEN FOWLER

**Andrews McMeel
Publishing**

Kansas City

www.andrewsmcmeel.com

Library of Congress Cataloging-in-Publication Data
    Fowler, Stephen.
      Millennium mania : fascinating facts and quotes
for the dawn of the 21st century / Stephen Fowler.
        p. cm.
     ISBN: 0-8362-6976-4
     1. Twenty-first century—Forecasts—Miscellanea.
2. Millennium—Miscellanea. I. Title
CB161.F59 1998
303.49'09'05—dc21   98–15896
                                         CIP

The following pages are a simple snapshot: a portrait, painted with trivia, of our collective mind at the cusp of the millennium. The extremes of behavior, the popular notions, the odd facts, the enthusiasms and gruff denials that surround this arbitrary, yet strangely urgent, event are thrown together here just as they are encountered in the world: without any pretense of order or context. Make of this madness what you will.

Stephen Fowler
February 1998

Stephen Fowler: www.sirius.com/~sfowler

Millennium: A period
of one thousand years. Also, a thousandth
anniversary.

—The Oxford English Dictionary

> **"I** think it's clear that perceptions are going to be distorted at the approach of the year 2000. It's a really juicy time."
>
> —*Richard Landes, director,*
> *Center for Millennial Studies*

The first formal preparations for acknowledging the millennium were made in 1963. That year, the World Association for Celebrating Year 2000 was founded in England by John Goodman, a self-employed printer. Unfortunately, Mr. Goodman did not live to see his work through to fruition—he died in 1994.

New Year's Eve 1999—
the night that promises to be the biggest
party of the century—falls on a Friday.

> *"The only certainty is that 2000 is bringing with it an astonishing set of predictions, fears, plans, hopes, and just plain nonsense."*

> —Bill Tammeus,
> Kansas City Star

In November 1996, Pope John Paul II announced plans for the "Great Jubilee 2000," a yearlong holy celebration by the Catholic Church to commemorate the two thousandth birthday of Jesus Christ.

The new millennium may bring a very real apocalypse—for computers. The "year 2000 bug" could prove to be a serious problem for antiquated machines programmed to count years in only two digits. When '99 rolls over to '00, such systems will mistake the new date for the year 1900.

The single most important event of the second millennium, according to *LIFE* magazine: "Gutenberg prints the Bible."

In Russia, the citizens of Moscow will recognize the millennium by inaugurating their recently rebuilt cathedral. The huge church is a replica of one destroyed during Stalin's reign, and its completion coincides conveniently with the two thousandth birthday of the savior it honors.

*"**M**illennium is spelled like this: M-I-L-L-E-N-N-I-U-M. It has two l's and two n's."*

—Barry Newman,
Wall Street Journal (1997)

*"**T**he world of the year 2000 has already arrived, for in the decisions we make now, in the way we design our environment and thus sketch the lines of constraints, the future is committed."*

—*sociologist Daniel Bell, 1968*

Thousands of sites across the World Wide Web are now enabled with "countdown clocks," which inform viewers precisely how many days, hours, and seconds remain

until the year 2000. Some of these clocks are even optimistically designed to start their job over after January 1, 2000, and begin the countdown to New Year's, 3000.

"*As the present century draws to a close we see looming not very far ahead the venerable dispute which reappears every hundred years: When does the next century begin?*"

—New York Times, *1896*

*"**A**ll those folks who are predicting events from waves of transcendence to prophecies of doom as we enter the year 2000 are going to have a rude awakening when nothing happens—apart from some wild parties and computer snafus."*

—psychologist Robert R. Butterworth

Officials in Paris have installed an illuminated millennium countdown clock on the Eiffel Tower.

Geek-speak: Computer programmers and industry insiders typically refer to the "year 2000 computer bug" in abbreviated form as "Y2K." Y stands for year; 2 for two; and K for kilo (the Greek-derived prefix for one thousand).

"**I**n the short term, writers and artists should resist the urge to produce works on millennial themes. There are already several thousand in the pipeline."

—*the London* Independent

On December 31, 1999, the festivities in Times Square are set to begin at 7 A.M.—midnight at the international date line. Organizers plan to celebrate straight through for twenty-four hours, until the millennium has passed in each of the twenty-four time zones of the world.

The original Christian idea of a "millennium," as described by St. John in Revelation 20, is the period of one thousand years leading up to the Last Judgment—a time during which Christ will reign on Earth with the resurrected souls of Christian martyrs.

The millennial change of A.D. 1000 saw the rise of the "Peace of God" movement in France and elsewhere in Europe. Peasants gathered by the thousands in fields and pastures to hold revival meetings that lasted for days.

The millennial festivities in Great Britain are being paid for in a novel way: After the creation of a national lottery in the 1990s, the government set aside 20 percent of lottery revenues for millennial expenses. The resulting fund is reported to have reached 1.6 billion pounds—that's a lot of noisemakers.

Where will the first ray of dawn fall on the first morning of the next millennium? Depends on whom you ask. The Pacific island nations of Kiribati, Fiji, Tonga, and New Zealand—all located near the international date line—have each laid claim to the honor.

Science fiction author Arthur C. Clarke proposed, in a 1973 interview, that mankind declare "the whole of 2000 a holiday. If we make it to there, we'll be fully justified."

The citizens of Berlin will welcome the year 2000 with an immense fireworks display—possibly the largest in history—at the Brandenberg Gate. The city's mayor, Eberhard Diepgen, said the celebration would symbolize "openness and change."

In 1996, a consulting firm called the Gartner Group warned Congress that the worldwide cost of correcting the year 2000 computer crisis would total some $600 billion.

> "*For most people, millennium events will just be a bigger version of annual New Year's Eve bashes. But not everyone will be in an up mood. Some fundamentalists, pop-culture prophets, and New Age adherents are anticipating a day of reckoning.*"
>
> —*John Yemma*, Boston Globe, *1997*

"It'll be the greatest party the world has ever seen."

—*Steve Leber, chairman of New York's Celebration 2000 committee, describing the city's plans for December 31, 1999*

The word "millennium" was first used in its modern, secular sense by English poet Thomas Ken in his work *Hymnarium*, published in 1721: "They on one Theme Millenniums spend."

*"**L**ord Jesus,
Lord of History,
Who came at the fullness of time,
prepare our hearts
to celebrate with faith
the great Jubilee of the Year 2000,
that it may be a year of grace
and mercy."*

—Pope John Paul II

*"**O**ne third of the world will care significantly, one third will notice it, and one third will barely be aware of it."*

—historian Peter Stearns, on the advent of the third Christian millennium

The first Christian chronology was created in the sixth century by a monk named Dionysius Exiguus (Dennis the Short), at the request of Pope St. John I. Dennis named the first year of the

Christian era "year one" rather than "year zero"—and set the stage for a long-running debate that still continues today: Does a new century begin in '00, or '01?

The term *fin de siècle*—French for "end of the century"—was first adopted into popular speech around the year 1885. The phrase was used to describe the decadent attitudes of the era.

British festivities for the millennial rollover will be centered in the London suburb of Greenwich, on the River Thames. The town is the site of the original Royal Greenwich Observatory, origin-point of the earth's Prime (or Greenwich) Meridian, and—in the words of Prime Minister Tony Blair— "the home of Time."

A Florida lawyer is offering New Year's enthusiasts a chance to celebrate the millennial rollover *four* times—by chartering an Air France Concorde. His party begins in Paris, then skips westward across the time zones to Newfoundland, then Vancouver, and finally Hawaii. Ticket price: $65,000.

Life in the year 2000—a prediction:

"Virus infections will still be rampant through their tendency to modify themselves to meet new treatments."

—New York Times Magazine, *1954*

As the two thousandth birthday of Jesus approaches, the city of Nazareth is bracing itself for a flood of pilgrims. According to the Holy Land Foundation, twenty-five to thirty million people are expected to visit the Messiah's "hometown" between 1998 and 2000.

> *"**T**here have been endtimes aplenty in the six thousand years of recorded history, but none so universal or so dangerous. . . . Be not deceived. Our twentieth-century endtime does surpass, in scope and destructive potential, all others."*

—*Warren Wagar,* Terminal Visions *(1982)*

Advance booking: Seattle's Space Needle was reserved nine years ahead of time for the night of December 31, 1999.

> ## *"It is clear that the start of the new millennium will be 1 January 2001."*

—*from a formal public statement issued by England's Royal Greenwich Observatory, in response to a glut of inquiries*

"**B**y the year 2020, there will be a whole new industry built on remembering the year 2000."

—*author Alvin Toffler*

New Year's celebrants in Iceland will
usher in the new millennium
by setting bonfires.

President Bill Clinton on the Y2K
computer bug:
"We can't have the American people
looking to a new century and a new
millennium with their computers—

the very symbol of modernity and the modern age—holding them back. And we're determined to see that it doesn't happen."

On the one thousandth anniversary of the founding of Rome—A.D. 247 by the Christian calendar—the Roman empire celebrated its millennium by slaughtering animals in the Circus Maximus and staging theatrical events for three consecutive nights.

A travel agency called Destinations 2000 is offering a "Countdown to the Millennium" package for casino enthusiasts. A chartered jet will carry the gamblers from Las Vegas to New Zealand and back again across the international date line, allowing these high-rollers a chance to experience New Year's Eve 1999 twice—both times in a casino.

The international date line, which determines where and when the first morning of the new millennium will dawn, is established by international custom. Neither the United Nations nor any other international authority has the right to prescribe its exact location.

"Experts estimate that by the year 2000 there will be more than eighty million cellular phones in use across the globe."

—Wired *magazine, 1995*

The United Nations has proclaimed
the year 2000 to be an "International Year
of Thanksgiving."

L

By late 1997, the United States Patent and Trademark Office had registered more than one hundred trademarks including the word "millennium," and over 1,500 containing the number "2000."

"*Our millennial Zeitgeist is obsessed with decline and fall. The instrument may be the computer, it may be nuclear war or virus or space aliens, but all of it pushes toward an end that annihilates the old and clears the way for ... what?*"

—Patt Morrison,
Los Angeles Times Magazine (1997)

As an exposition center for its Greenwich 2000 celebration, Great Britain is building the largest dome ever constructed. The structure, 164 feet high and more than a half-mile in circumference, will be large enough to hold 3,300 double-decker buses.

> "*Experts speak of chaos enveloping New Zealand, where the millennium dawns first, then advancing like a wave across the world.*"

—London's Sunday Times,
describing the possible effects of the Y2K computer bug

New Year's Eve is not a raucous event in Japan. According to a recent poll, 42 percent of Japanese under age sixty plan to spend the evening of December 31, 1999, at home.

"There's a growing excitement about the idea that we will be living in a rare, historical moment—the conclusion of a century and the birth of a millennium.

No matter where we are in the country, the celebrations of the millennium will reflect the creativity, diversity, and raw energy of Americans."

—*Hillary Rodham Clinton*

The initials in the term "A.D. 2000" stand for *Anno Domini*—Latin for "Year of Our Lord." The term was introduced by Dennis the Short, a sixth-century monk who created the first Christian calendar.

The year 2000 will be the 1,200th anniversary of the crowning of Charlemagne as Europe's Holy Roman Emperor.

Life in the year 2000—a prediction:

"*T*he rocket letter post will make possible return mail to Australia in a single day."

—New York Times Magazine, *December 26, 1954*

LX

It is the stated goal of the Clinton administration to have every classroom and library in America connected to the Internet by the year 2000.

> **"I** cannot understand how people can be found to maintain that a century does not begin until the end of its first year."

—*Lord Medway, writing to the editor of the London Times, January, 1900*

According to Mark Kingwell, author of *Dreams of Millennium: Report from a Culture on the Brink,* some 350 apocalyptic cults worldwide are predicting an Armageddon of one sort or another in the year 2000.

Citizens of Panama will be celebrating more than just the millennium on December 31, 1999. That's the day the U.S. hands over control of the Panama Canal to the Panamanians.

The first Y2K lawsuit was filed in August 1997, by a Michigan grocery. Produce Palace International found that its electronic cash registers would shut down every time a checker processed a customer's credit card with an expiration date of year 2000 or later. The grocery is suing its point-of-sale system provider for unspecified damages.

> "*The millennium affects people the way moonlight affects werewolves, the way sirens affect dogs, the way that bizarre black monolith affected the apes in 2001.*"

—*Peter Carlson*

"*I found myself between two centuries, as at the confluence of two rivers. I plunged into their troubled waters, regretfully distancing myself from the old shore on which I was born, swimming hopefully toward an unknown bank.*"

—*Vicomte François René de Chateaubriand, describing the transition from the 1700s to the 1800s*

Catholics in America will contribute to the spirit of their church's "Great Jubilee 2000" when they inaugurate the Pope John Paul II Cultural Center in Washington that year. The center will serve as a U.S. branch of the Vatican museum, as well as a theological study center.

English: millennium
French: millénaire
Italian: millennio
Spanish: milenio
Danish: årtusinde
Czech: tisíciletí
Esperanto: miljaro

"**T**he average 1971 West Georgia freshman will be only forty-seven years old in the year 2000. Will he or she be able to look back to our curriculum and say, 'They gave me the skills I needed to survive in a world *of radical change,' or will our alumnus look back and charge, 'They taught me the wisdom of the past but ignored the problems of the future'?"*

—Newt Gingrich, "Some Projections on West Georgia College's Next 30 Years" (1971)

*"**N**ow is the watershed of Cosmic history. We stand at the threshold of the New Millennium. Behind us yawn the chasms of the primordial past, when this universe was a dead and silent place; before us rise the broad sunlit uplands of a living cosmos."*

—*Marshall T. Savage,* The Millennial Project: Colonizing the Galaxy in 8 Easy Steps *(1997)*

Just days before the world celebrates the millennial rollover, the island of Macao will experience a rollover of its own. After 150 years of Portuguese rule, Macao becomes a "special administrative region" of China on December 20, 1999.

According to the journal of England's Royal Geographical Society, the first inhabited patch of the earth to be touched by the dawn of the new millennium will be Hakepa Hill on New Zealand's Pitt Island.

*"**T**he millennium is already showing signs of becoming a massive retrospective of where we have been, not where we are going. This makes a certain amount of sense. Having broken through the pane of the future, we're in a bit of a void."*

—*Paul O'Donnell*, Washington Post *(1997)*

"*In the year 1000, most people thought the world was coming to an end but that God would do it and that the faithful would be rewarded in the kingdom of heaven. Today, we have the capacity to destroy ourselves*

in a way we never did before. If we put an end to the world, there will be no redemption."

—Richard Landes, director,
Center for Millennial Studies

The New Year's Eve 1999 Celebration in Times Square will be hosted by ageless television icon Dick Clark, and is expected to attract 250 million viewers worldwide.

In addition to the millennium, the citizens of Samoa will also celebrate a centenary anniversary in the year 2000— that year will be their one hundredth as an American territory.

A.D. 2000 will also mark the one thousandth anniversary of the first visit to the New World by Viking navigator Leif Erikson.

*"**I**ronically, while the Apocalypse they prophesy has never come, in more pedestrian terms, millennialists often succeed: The world is a different place after them. It really was the end of the world as we'd known it."*

—from the Center for Millennial Studies web site

On December 31, 1999, the Arc de Triomphe in Paris will be temporarily turned into an immense timepiece. The twelve avenues that radiate out from the monument will be lit in sequence like the minute and hour hands of a clock, aligning at midnight down the city's most celebrated avenue, the Champs Elysées.

Word's out: In January of 1997, the word "millennium" could be found on some 30,000 web pages worldwide. A year later, that number had leaped to more than 217,000—a staggering 723 percent increase.

"*The stage is somewhat empty at this point. After the millennium, it will be time for a set designer to invent an early twenty-first-century vision of the future.*"

—science fiction author Bruce Sterling, quoted in the Washington Post *(1997)*

Life in the year 2000—a prediction:

"No specific subjects will be taught in schools; education will consist of games and occupational therapy."

—New York Times Magazine, *1954*

In the year 2000, Bill and Hillary Clinton will celebrate their twenty-fifth wedding anniversary.

Most scholars believe that Dennis the Short—the sixth-century monk who established a Christian timeline based on the birth of Christ—miscalculated by four to seven years. Christ was probably born in the year 4 B.C. . . . before himself?!?!

Sigmund Freud, whose *Interpretation of Dreams* was published in late 1899, wrote on January 8, 1900: "The new century, the most interesting thing about which for us may be that it contains the dates of our deaths, has brought me nothing but a stupid review in the *Zeit*."

New Year's Scrooges wishing to skip the millennial rollover entirely can reserve a ticket on Qantas Air flight 8, scheduled to depart Los Angeles at 12:50 A.M. on December 31, 1999. Flying west across the international date line, the flight arrives in Sydney, Australia, late at night on January 1—without ever having experienced a midnight transition into the year 2000.

In 1996, the U.S. government predicted that three hundred man-years of work would be required to protect the computers of just one of its departments—the Internal Revenue Service—from the year 2000 bug.

"*Millennial prophets today bear little resemblance to the cartoon caricature of the bearded, white-robed figure with the picket sign proclaiming that 'The End is Near.' They can be found in business suits, at church, at work, on television, and on the Internet.*"

—Stephen D. O'Leary, "Heaven's Gate and the Culture of Popular Millennialism" (1997)

> **"*I* want it to be fun; I want it to be entertaining, but I also want it to be an opportunity for people to reflect on who we are, what sort of society we live in and where we're going as a country."**

—Peter Mandelson, British government supervisor of the Millennium Dome project

The difference between a "millennium" and a "chiliad"? None whatsoever. Both words mean "a period of one thousand years"—the former from Latin, the latter from Greek.

"*Centuries and millennia are always arbitrary: You don't need to be a medievalist to know that. However, it's true that syndromes of decadence or rebirth can form around such symbolic divisions of time.*"

—*Italian scholar and novelist Umberto Eco*

The highlight of the millennial year in Australia promises to be the games of the XXVII Olympiad, set to take place in Sydney from September 15 to October 1, 2000.

According to a definition agreed upon at the International Meridian Conference in 1884, each day on Earth begins precisely at midnight in Greenwich, England. Which means, technically speaking, that a New Year's celebration in New York—five time zones west of Greenwich—should be observed at 7 P.M., December 31.

The year A.D. 1000 witnessed a rash of "heresies" preached in France, Italy, and the southwestern Mediterranean. The eleventh-century monk Radulphus Glaber interpreted these events as the unleashing of Satan, as written in the Book of Revelation.

As her tribute to the millennium, artist Adrienne Sioux Koopersmith of Chicago is attempting to date a different man every night for two thousand days leading up to the year 2000. She intends to then select the most qualified candidate of the two thousand, and marry him in Times Square as the ball drops and the millennium turns.

On May 5, 2000, an unusual grouping of the Moon and the five "naked eye" planets will take place in the heavens. Don't bother digging your telescope out of the closet, though; astronomers predict that Earth's view of the "planetary alignment" will be blocked by another celestial object—the Sun.

The landmark science fiction film *Metropolis,* made by German director Fritz Lang in 1926, portrayed a world of miserable workers enslaved by a heartless technocracy. The picture was set in the year 2000.

The millennial world's fair, Expo 2000, will be held in Hannover, Germany, and organizers are predicting upward of forty million visitors. More than 150 nations are planning to participate, and the event's broadly inclusive theme—"Mankind, Nature, and Technology"—should offer something for everyone.

According to *The Semantic Rhyming Dictionary*, there is no perfect rhyme for the word "millennium."

> **"I** want to put together a festival that will raise the consciousness of the world, something spiritual for people of all races and denominations to laugh, dance, and cry at the same time."

—musician Carlos Santana, on his plans for
December 31, 1999

"**W**e came from the Level Above Human in distant space and we have now exited the bodies that we were wearing for our earthly task . . . We came for the purpose of offering a

CIV

doorway to the Kingdom of God at the end of this civilization, the end of this millennium."

—from the final statement issued by the Heaven's Gate cult before their mass suicide in Rancho Santa Fe, California

In 1996, the nation of Kiribati—a group of thirty-three islands straddling the international date line in the South Pacific—declared itself to be entirely to the west of the date line. Based on this technicality, Caroline Island, the most easterly of the Kiribati chain, may now be the first land to be touched by the dawn of January 1, 2000.

*"**T**he Big 2000 might be capitalism's best invention since Christmas."*

—Tom Huth, *on the merchandising of the millennium,
in* Fortune *magazine*

Compared to its European neighbors, Belgium will celebrate the millennium quietly. Its national budget for millennial festivities is $38 million—less than 5 percent of what England will spend on its "Millennium Dome" alone.

The "millennium bug" first stung American taxpayers in January of 1998. Due to an error by programmers working to clear IRS computers of the Y2K glitch, approximately one thousand people were incorrectly declared to be in default on their tax installment agreements.

Turn-of-the-century festivities planned in Paris for December 31, 1900, had to be canceled due to bad weather; one hundred thousand francs, which otherwise would have paid for party expenses, were donated to the poor.

A 1997 "Comfort Barometer" poll commissioned by shoe manufacturer Rockport asked a sampling of Americans, "How comfortable are you with the direction of your own life as we enter the new millennium?" Forty-nine percent of respondents claimed to be "very comfortable;" only 4 percent admitted to being "very uncomfortable."

Q. Why didn't Dennis the Short include the year zero in the Christian chronology he created in the sixth century?

A. Because the concept of "zero" wasn't accepted into European mathematics until the 12th century A.D.— poor Dennis never even knew what he was missing.

During the millennial rollover of A.D. 1000, many of Europe's Christians believed that a prophesied thousand-year peace would begin with the unification and reform of the Eastern and Western branches of their church. Despite the best efforts of Holy Roman Emperor Otto III, however, this was not to be; Otto was poisoned in 1002 by his Roman mistress Stephania.

In Dublin, Ireland, a six-ton underwater clock—the "Countdown 2000 Millennium Timer"—was installed in the Liffey River in 1996. Due to the river's murky water, however, one local journalist complained that the sight was "like inviting your guests to admire the family silver when it was floating in a greasy sink."

Because so many customers of British recording label Millennium Records were unable to spell its name correctly—and therefore unable to look up its web site— the company established a second site, this time using the popular "Millenium" misspelling.

"The Heaven's Gate web pages declare that we are in the 'End of the Age' and that the earth is soon to be swept clean of civilization. The disturbing truth about this group's *suicide is that the members are far from atypical in their anticipation of end times and catastrophe."*

—Stephen D. O'Leary, *"Heaven's Gate and the Culture of Popular Millennialism" (1997)*

M&M's "Red" and "Yellow"—two animated talking candies—claimed the role of "official spokescandies of the millennium" in early 1998. As the package says, "MM means 2000"— in Roman numerals.

The antiquated computer language Cobol, created in the 1960s by several computer manufacturers in collaboration with the U.S. Department of Defense, is responsible for the most widely spread Y2K fears. Mainframes in critical businesses and government positions around the world still depend on it.

"*About the only thing we agree on is that the future is coming in a big round number, and that it's making us anxious and exhilarated in equal measure.*"

—New Statesman, 1996

As part of their city's millennial festivities, planners in Paris have announced that a guitar festival in honor of Jimi Hendrix will be held at a Parisian racetrack in the year 2000.

*"**T**hose of us who care about truth have already started cringing in the expectation that millions of ignorant fools will celebrate the start of the third millennium in the wrong year."*

—*irritable Jan Wikstrom, who insists that the next millennium begins in 2001, writing in the* Sydney Bulletin *(1996)*

In a 1984 study, a group of Colorado school children were asked to write an essay describing life in their state in the year 2001. Nearly half the essays predicted a world struggling in the aftermath of an apocalyptic World War III.

Saatchi & Saatchi Advertising tracked consumer attitudes toward the millennium for more than two years in the mid-1990s. A typical everyman response to their poll: "I don't think about it very much, and when I do, it seems to me that it will be just another day in my life."

The Pacific islands nation of Kiribati is so eager to be "first into the millennium" that its government has renamed its most easterly point. The uninhabited rock formerly known as Caroline Island is now officially Millennium Island.

On the literal eve of the twentieth century—December 31, 1900—the Christian Pentecostal movement was founded in Topeka, Kansas, when a classroom of Bible students discovered the gift of speaking in tongues.

In 1995, the Dutch newspaper *NRC Handelsblad* organized a competition for proposals of public projects to celebrate the new millennium. But by 1997, after reviewing many hundreds of submissions, the dissatisfied contest jury concluded that none of the proposals was worthy of a first prize.

*S*yndicated columnist Dave Barry
on the Y2K bug:
"Experts tell us that if it is not fixed,
when the year 2000 arrives, our
telephone system will be unreliable,
our financial records will be

inaccurate, our government will be paralyzed and airline flights will be canceled without warning. In other words, things will be pretty much as they are now."

Looking ahead to the millennium from January 1998, the *Christian Science Monitor* claimed that 35 percent of Americans believe "it's possible that a battle of Armageddon is coming."

> *"It will be an extraordinary, absurd, almost blasphemous thing if Britain chooses to commemorate the two thousandth birthday of Jesus Christ with a nationalized version of Mickey Mouse, paid for from the profits of gambling."*
>
> —editorial in the London Daily Telegraph, January 1998, referring to the planned celebrations at the "Millennium Dome"

In early 1997, a study by the *Washington Post* calculated how many articles about the upcoming millennial rollover had appeared in the nation's leading newspapers. It found 335 in 1992; 503 in 1994; and 889 in 1996.

> *"The end of the millennium is an unsettling time, very nervous-making. . . . I got this idea that someone should be making money on it."*

—*Chris Carter, creator of* The X-Files *and* Millennium *on Fox Television*

Builders in Luxembourg are rushing to complete their country's first modern art museum by the year 2000. Luxembourgers hope that the Grand Duke Museum of Modern Art, designed by architect I.M. Pei, will make their tiny nation a prominent player on Europe's cultural landscape in the next millennium.

The United States does not have an official calendar, nor does it legally require adherence to any calendar in particular. Nevertheless, popular consensus unanimously favors the Gregorian (or Christian Era) calendar.

*"**C**oncerning the end of the world, as a youth I heard a sermon in a church in Paris that as soon as the number of a thousand years should come, the Antichrist would come, and not long thereafter, the Last Judgment would follow."*

—*Abbo of Fleury, circa* A.D. *996*

In December of 1999, the members of the Millennium Society of Washington, D.C., will sail for Egypt on the Queen Elizabeth II. They plan to hold—and televise via satellite—their millennial gala at the Great Pyramid of Cheops on December 31. Note: The pyramid itself is more than twice as old as the anniversary being celebrated there.

A 1997 study by the British government indicated that many hospitals, lagging in Y2K computer preparation, might be forced to close their doors to all but the most extreme emergency cases come January 2000.

Life in the year 2000—a prediction:

*" **A** Channel tunnel will connect England and France. "*

—New York Times Magazine, *1954*

The Israeli city of Bethlehem—the birthplace of Jesus and an obvious destination for Christian pilgrims at the time of his two thousandth birthday—is currently under the control of the Palestinian Authority. The Palestinians, scrambling to improve tourist facilities in the ancient town, are hoping for $55 million in assistance from the World Bank.

One Chicago organization, in an effort to distinguish itself from all the other millennial-events organizers, has coined its own name for the big rollover. The Billennium Organizing Committee has registered the word "billennium" as a trademark worldwide.

The *Fortean Times*, a British journal that tracks bizarre and uncanny phenomena, found a distinct increase in the media's coverage of weird behavior in 1997. "Although I don't make prophecies, I wouldn't be surprised if the index didn't continue upwards as a result of pre-millennial tension," said Joe McNally, associate editor.

As part of the White House Millennium Project, Hillary Clinton has organized a series of lectures to be delivered at the executive mansion. The first speaker to appear at one of these "millennium evenings" was Harvard historian Bernard Bailyn; the second will be physicist Stephen Hawking.

January 1, 2000, will also fall on the year 1421—according to the traditional Islamic lunar calendar.

In its review of a recent book, *Fins de Siècle: How Centuries End,* the *Economist Review* had this to say: "The title is a bit of a cheat. These seven essays examine the turn of each century from 1400 to 2000, only to show that centuries end in no special way."

Denmark plans to welcome the year 2000 with nationwide pyrotechnics. Displays of fireworks in all 275 of the country's administrative districts will be linked via computer network and set off simultaneously.

Central Boiler of Greenbush, Minnesota, manufactures a gas log fireplace boiler called the Millennium 2100.

The year 2000 will mark the five hundredth anniversary of the discovery of Brazil by Portuguese seafarer Pedro Alvares Cabral.

For celebrants seeking advance information and news updates on New York's millennial festivites, the city has established a special "Millennium Club." Membership is twenty dollars.

In the year 1900, Pablo Picasso completed a painting called *La Fin du Numéro* (End of the Number).

The hard-to-spell Millennium Society of Washington, D.C., has received membership applications addressed to:

The Melanium Society
The Millenneum Society
The Millionian Society
The Millinial Society
The Malanuim Society

CLI

The nine "cultural capitals" designated by the European Union to "represent Europe in the year 2000": Avignon, France; Bergen, Norway; Bologna, Italy; Brussels, Belgium; Helsinki, Finland; Krakow, Poland; Prague, Czech Republic; Reykjavik, Iceland; and Santiago de Compostela, Spain.

*"**E**very proponent of 2001 makes the same argument: Although the idea that a century begins on the 00 year may stem from an intuitive, odometric logic, it betrays the public's lack of mathematical sophistication."*

—*Dick Terisi*, Atlantic Monthly *(1997)*

"*As we approach the end of the millennium, we can assume that there will be more bizarre incidents and gruesome deaths, either in anticipation of prophetic fulfillment or in the aftermath of apocalyptic disappointment.*"

—*Stephen D. O'Leary, "Heaven's Gate and the Culture of Popular Millennialism" (1997)*

Developers David Hosea and Wayne Carlisle hope to complete a "Millennium Tower" in Newport, Kentucky, by December 31, 1999. The planned structure would be the world's eleventh tallest tower, and would contain a sixty-six-thousand-pound free-swinging bell and the world's largest clock.

The Y2K problem has proven to be a windfall for older programmers—they're the only ones familiar with the outdated computer languages affected by the bug. One consulting company, desperate to find qualified programmers, even placed an ad in *Modern Maturity*, the magazine of the AARP.

> *"For one hundred years and more, we have looked fearfully toward 1999 as the year of unappealable verdicts, then hopefully toward 2000 as the year of pardon and jubilee."*
>
> —*Hillel Schwartz,* Century's End *(1990)*

Une omelette, madame? French festival organizers are designing a giant "egg" to be "laid" by the Eiffel Tower at midnight on New Year's Eve, 1999. While two thousand drums roll, the egg will crack open to reveal hundreds of television monitors tuned to millennial festivities around the world.

The Anno Domini system created by Dennis the Short was not widely known until A.D. 731, when it was employed by a Northumbrian monk named Bede in his landmark work, *The Ecclesiastical History of the English People.*

In the late 1960s, Newt Gingrich taught a course entitled, "The Year 2000: How Do You Think About the Future?" at Tulane University in New Orleans.

As part of the Catholic Church's Great Jubilee 2000, the Holy Shroud of Turin will be placed on public display for six weeks in 1998, and again for six weeks in 2000.

The Anno Domini chronology was first employed by a government bureaucracy during the reign of Holy Roman Emperor Charlemagne, A.D. 800–814.

In the year 1000, Viking strongman Olaf Tryggvesson convinced the people of Iceland, gathered together on the plains of Thingvellir, to convert to Christianity.

Austrian glassware manufacturer Riedel is offering a line of fluted crystal "Millennium Glasses" for champagne drinkers. The company will issue a new commemorative glass each year from 1998 through 2002, with the year's number cut into the crystal.

"It's ironic—we move forward and our computers move backward one hundred years."

—Rep. Constance A. Morella of Maryland, musing on the Y2K computer bug

"*For the last forty years or so, a lot of respectable divinity schools have shied away from talking about 'last things.' The millennium was discussed in psychological terms rather than as a great historical question for the churches.*"

—Rodney Peterson, director
of the Boston Theological Institute

Windows on the World, the restaurant at the top of New York's World Trade Center, took its first reservation for the night of December 31, 1999, all the way back in 1986.

In early 1998, the Miller Brewing Company applied for a trademark on the word "Millerennium."

According to the National Institute of Standards and Technology in Washington, D.C., the third millennium will begin on January 1, 2001.

> "*Millennial moments tend to make us look for ways to get on God's good side.*"

—Richard Landes, director, Center for
Millennial Studies

"*We have great hope for the millennium. It's a great opportunity for all sparkling wine customers to buy a celebratory bottle. And who knows, maybe we'll get two shots, in 2000 and 2001.*"

—*Eileen Crane, winemaker at the Domaine Carneros champagne cellars in Napa County, California*

Despite rumors to the contrary, the electronic calendars embedded in VCRs will not be affected by the Y2K computer bug. Most VCRs built before 1992 don't even measure years; those built more recently count years in four digits, and will have no problem with the 2000 turnover.

In the United States, at least two wrecking contractors use the word "millennium" in their company names.

"**B**y the coming of the third year after the year 1000, churches and buildings everywhere were again being rebuilt. . . . It was as if the very world was shaking itself rid of its decrepitude and everywhere put on a white mantle of churches."

—monk Radulphus Glaber of Burgundy, writing in the eleventh century

As part of the White House Millennium Program, the Smithsonian Institution will be hosting a Festival of American Folklife.

In January 1998, the Federal Aviation Administration announced it would tackle the Y2K problem head-on: first by de-bugging its current outdated computers, then replacing them with new ones for good measure. According to an FAA spokesperson, "We're trying to do both because it gives us the highest assurance and insurance."

New Year's Day, A.D. 2000, will also fall on the year 4697—according to the traditional Chinese lunar calendar.

On December 29, 1900, the Indianapolis *Recorder* ran a "New Year Reverie" of scientific prognostications for the twentieth century. Among its predictions: a train tunnel would be dug through the earth to China, and the Moon would be divided up among the world's nations.

In Japan, people traditionally eat sticky rice cakes called *mochi* on New Year's Day. It's questionable whether this habit brings good luck, however: Every year a number of elderly Japanese choke to death on the glutinous substance.

The end of the twentieth century will mark the first time in history that the entire world has entered a new millennium together. Only since 1949 have all major nations used the Gregorian (or Christian Era) calendar for official datekeeping.

"*Apocalypticism is the province of the wretched, the downtrodden, the dispossessed, the political radical, the theological revolutionary, and the self-proclaimed savior—not the belief of people happily at the helm.*"

—*Stephen Jay Gould,*
Questioning the Millennium *(1997)*

Across the River Thames from London's Parliament buildings, the British are building a "Giant Millennium Ferris Wheel." At five hundred feet high, the Millennium Wheel will be the largest wheel of any kind ever built—and promises to entertain celebrants with a twenty-minute "flight."

Since at least 1963, pundits have been discussing what to call the year 2000 and the subsequent '00 decade. For Hayes B. Jacobs of the *New Yorker,* the answer was "Twenty oh-oh"—"a nervous name for what is sure to be a nervous year."

In Paris, festival organizers plan to pour perfume into the Seine River at the stroke of midnight, December 31, 1999.

"**A** lot of companies, when they found out how big the problem was, just went into a catatonic state."

—Y2K computer consultant Jim Wookward

"*Our time has something about it of the end of an epoch. One sign thereof is the disappearance of an elemental joy in historical reality.*"

—German philosopher Wilhelm Dilthey, writing at the close of the nineteenth century

A California group called Wright Thinking is hoping to ensure that the turn of the millennium is the most photographed and videotaped moment in history. Its "World Millennium Snapshot" project intends to compile millions of images snapped at the stroke of midnight into a "navigable holomorph database" for the sake of posterity.

A king with a real spike on his helmet: In 1899, Kaiser Wilhelm II of Germany courageously stood up to the world's pedants by announcing that the twentieth century would begin on January 1, 1900—*not* 1901.

Not a firecracker: On December 31, 1900, as celebrants ushered in the twentieth century, an anarchist bomber in Chicago attempted to blow up the La Salle Street tunnel.

British tycoon Richard Branson, founder of the Virgin entertainment and transportation empire, is planning to throw "the biggest street party in the world" in Edinburgh, Scotland, on December 31, 1999.

When the monk known as Dennis the Short established the Christian timeline in the sixth century, he chose January 1 as its first day. Not December 25 (the day of Christ's birth), but a week later—the day of Christ's ritual circumcision.

One bit of proof offered by Ted Daniels, author of the *Millennial Prophecy Report,* that the impending millennium is affecting people's minds: A London firm now sells insurance against "inadvertent intergalactic pregnancy"—for those who fear rape and impregnation by aliens.

The year 2000 is a census year in the United States. To improve the public's response rate to census questionnaires, the Census Bureau is paying an ad agency $100 million to spread the word about its millennial head-count.

According to the *Boston Business Journal,* some five hundred outdated software packages still widely in use at the end of the century will need to be rewritten to prevent a year 2000 data disaster.

> "What the last decade is to a century the last century is to a millennium, so far, therefore, from sighing for 1901, we ought to be positively dreading it, and 2001 ought to be as great a relief as was 1001."

—Atlantic Monthly, *1891*

The people of Germany will celebrate the arrival of the millennium by re-inaugurating Berlin as their nation's capital. After an absence of more than fifty years, the German parliament will return to a reconstructed Reichstag in Berlin in the year 2000.

The trademarked term "Millennium Celebrations" belongs to a marketing firm in Oakbrook Terrace, Illinois.

Life in the year 2000—a prediction:

"*F*amily life will have been revived by television."

—New York Times Magazine, *1954*

Peter Mandelson, the British government minister responsible for the millennial festivities in Greenwich, England, had this to say about his country's gigantic "Millennium Dome": "We are constructing the most famous building in the world."

New Year's Day, A.D. 2000, will also fall on the year 5760—according to the traditional Jewish calendar.

The Magyar barbarian leader who subdued Hungary in A.D. 997 was the first king of that country to convert to Christianity. He even postponed his coronation until the year 1000, to honor the millennial anniversary of Christ's birth.

*"**I**'d like you to imagine thousands of school children lining the shoreline, perhaps spaced no more than two meters apart, all simultaneously lighting their coconut-sheath torches on the stroke of midnight."*

—*a marketing representative for the nation of Tonga (one of several Pacific islands claiming to be "first into the millennium")*

By early 1997, large companies were already experiencing problems as a result of the year 2000 computer bug. Defense contractor Lockheed Martin, for instance, ran into problems in April of that year while preparing five-year projections for the Defense Department.

Third Millennium Research of Seattle offers services as futuristic as its name: It preserves customers' DNA for cryonic resurrection at some time in the distant future.

As part of New York City's millennial celebrations, a parade of tall ships is being planned for July 4, 2000. Ships representing more than fifty nations will gather in New York Harbor for "Op Sail 2000," and organizers estimate that the parade may stretch across ten miles of water.

Q: What will people call the decade following the year 2000?

A: The "aughts," "aughties," "deucies," "double ohs," "hundreds," "M's," "naughts," "naughties," "ohs," "20-tens," "zeroes," "zilches," or "zips."

*"**W**e often celebrate to hide our fears, which is why we'll celebrate the millennium."*

—*psychologist Joyce Brothers*

"*Getting a luxury stay fixed at this stage is going to mean stepping into a dead man's shoes.*"

—*anonymous hotel owner in Edinburgh, Scotland, speaking in 1997 about the difficulty of reserving hotel rooms for New Year's Eve, 1999*

"*The present century will not terminate till January 1, 1801. . . . We shall not pursue this question further. . . . It is a silly, childish discussion, and only exposes the want of brains of those who maintain a contrary opinion to that we have stated.*"

—*the* Times *of London, December 26, 1799*

The year 2000 will mark the 250th anniversary of the death of Johann Sebastian Bach.

If you can remember the turn of the *last* century, you're invited to the Omni Shoreham Hotel in Washington, D.C., for New Year's Eve 1999. Centurians only, please; folks under one hundred years old need not apply.

As of January 1998, American Express had not issued a single credit card with an expiration date past December 1999. The rationale? The company hoped to protect its cardholders from possible Y2K problems.

"*Greedy people will stay in the third dimension, unable to access higher information.*"

—*a prediction for the year 2000 by Shala Mattingly, a "past-life therapist"*

French Champagne producer Louis Roederer is bottling two thousand "methuselahs"—each the equivalent of eight standard bottles—in honor of the millennial rollover. The wine, a 1990 vintage, won't last as long as its biblical namesake, who supposedly lived 969 years.

By November of 1997, the U.S. Patent and Trademark Office had received nearly eighty applications for trademarks using the word "millenium"—spelled with only one "n."

"For centuries, Armageddon has meant an end-times battle of horrific proportions. As the end of the millennium approaches, it also means tourists for Israel."

—Kansas City Star, *February 22, 1997*

An opinion poll conducted in late 1997 showed that 80 percent of British subjects were opposed to the construction of the Greenwich "Millennium Dome," and would prefer that the project be scrapped and its funding be redirected.

For those concerned with historical accuracy regarding the date of Christ's birth, Professor Glen Bowersock of the Institute for Advanced Study in Princeton, New Jersey, offers this suggestion: "Just remember the jingle— 'Hark the herald angels roar, Christ was born in B.C. four.'"

> "As the end of the millennium approaches, Sting doesn't mind sounding more like someone from the '60s than someone from the '90s."

—San Diego Union-Tribune, *March 10, 1996*

Birthday suit for the millennium: On the last night of 1999, Sydney, Australia will host a daring "bachelors and spinsters ball" on its Bondi beach. Dress is strictly black tie: no other clothing allowed.

"*A* new century is to a nation very much what a new year is to a man."

—*poet Paul Valéry, December 1900*

"After Christie Brinkley toured Nu Skin International's headquarters in downtown Provo a few months ago, she asked a question that floored the firm's computer systems manager.

'By the way,' asked the super model who pitches the company's beauty products, *'what is Nu Skin doing about Y2K?'"*

—*Salt Lake City's* Deseret News, *November 10, 1997*

As the century draws to a close, the U.S. Postal Service plans to issue ten sets of commemorative stamps, one for each decade of the 1900s. For the first time ever, the Postal Service will invite the American people to submit ideas for the stamps' subject matter.

When the first light of the third millennium dawns on the south Pacific, the tourists and islanders gathered there to watch it may get a soaking: January is hurricane season in that region.

Out with the old, in with the new: According to medieval monk Radulphus Glaber of Burgundy, during the few years prior to A.D. 1000, "in Italy and Gaul were seen to die all the most eminent prelates, dukes, and counts."

Underwater festivities: On December 31, 1999, England's Millennium Train Company will haul 1,600 passengers—800 from London, 800 from Paris—deep into the "Chunnel" beneath the English Channel for a "spectacular" midnight celebration.

Devout Muslims may not have anything to fear from the year A.D. 2000, but they do foresee trouble a bit farther down the timeline. Mohammed predicted a "Day of Doom" would occur in fifty thousand years.

Running an Internet search on the word "millennium," researchers at advertising magazine *Brandweek* were disturbed to find that a site called "The Millennium Project" yielded only one huge word on the screen: "Forbidden."

How the calendar invaded the news
magazines: In early 1997,
Newsweek began running a weekly
future-watch column called
"2000: The Millennium Notebook."

According to the Gartner Group, a technology consulting firm, the Y2K computer problem led to the accidental release of several inmates from an unnamed U.S. state prison in 1996. The prison's computer mistook the convicts' release dates as set for early in the 1900s, not the 2000s.

> *"**T**he millennium is one of the most significant communications opportunities for churches."*
>
> —*Rev. Richard Thomas of the Churches' Advertising Network, Windsor, England*

On the first morning of the year 2000, many Japanese will climb Mount Fuji to witness the sun rise on the new millennium. They even have a specific word for the first sunrise of the year: *Hatsuhinode.*

"**I**n the present and future of every skin, there is a turning point—where it begins to appear tired, dry, and older-looking. But now there is an alternative. Millenium."

—*from a brochure for Elizabeth Arden's new "Millenium" line of (misspelled) skin-care products*

To acknowledge the millennial anniversary of the founding of Rome, the Roman Empire issued commemorative coins stamped with the profile of a hippopotamus.

The artist formerly known as Prince—who might prove to be the biggest celebrity of Millennium Eve, thanks to his 1982 hit song "1999"—has offered very few specifics about his plans for the big night: "We're just going to have a party, and invite everyone who's supported us."

*"**T**o insist on a definition of 'millennium' at odds with the understanding of the vast majority of our readers would require countless schoolmarmish footnotes that would be more likely to spread confusion than light."*

—Dave Favrot, Sacramento Bee *copy desk chief*

Tracy Williams, a clairvoyant from Rockville Centre, New York, predicts "the cloning of teeth" will be achieved in the twenty-first century.

Austrian-Canadian businessman Frank Stronach is hoping to have his Globe Resort theme park near Vienna finished in time to celebrate New Year's Eve, 1999. The six-hundred-acre park will offer everything from an environmental institute to a track for horse racing, all overshadowed by an immense globe, 460 feet tall.

For businesses worried about the impending year 2000 computer crisis, insurance provider J & H Marsh & McLennan is offering a policy called "2000 Secure," which covers companies against the data disaster for up to $200 million.

Millennial consumers polled by Saatchi & Saatchi Advertising reported a distinct preference for the "old days" of the 1950s over the complexities and uncertainties of a post-2000 future.

To celebrate the "Great Jubilee 2000," the city of Rome hired architect Renzo Piano to build a massive auditorium containing three concert halls. Construction was interrupted when archaeological ruins were discovered on the site, but Piano redrew his plans to incorporate the ruins, and construction has gone forward.

Media survey: By August 1997, the *New York Times* had already identified what promises to be the cliché of the century. An electronic search of newspaper and magazine databases turned up hundreds, perhaps thousands, of articles containing the phrase "As we approach the millennium. . . . " The paper reprinted almost thirty examples, just to prove its point.

> *"**T**he true threat of millennial anxiety, the true apocalypse, is not the fire and brimstone promised in Revelation, the wailing and gnashing of teeth of Judgment Day. It is, instead, the destruction of hope, of faith in ourselves."*

—*Mark Kingwell,* Dreams of Millennium: Report from a Culture on the Brink *(1996)*

"**Y**ou can see it very early from such a height, probably at four A.M. There won't be any noise or crowds, just the sun rising over India. It will be beautiful."

—*Commander Jagindar Singh of Quest Tours, who plans to lead a small group of spiritual adventurers up the southern slope of the Himalayas to see the first dawn of the year 2000*

Crystal Cruise Lines is offering its customers the opportunity to experience the millennial rollover at the international date line, on the Pacific Ocean near the island of Tonga. The Florida-based company claims that its passengers will "be the last to leave 1999 and the first to see 2000."

> "*This dreadful gruesome New Year, so monstrously numbered, makes me turn back to the warm and colored past and away from the big black avenue that gapes in front of us.*"

—Henry James, 1900

Tim Kneeland of Seattle is celebrating the millennium with a yearlong bicycle rally. Participants in his "Odyssey 2000" will depart from Los Angeles on January 1, 2000, and spend a year circumnavigating the earth under pedal-power.

The composition popularly known as the "2001 Theme" from Stanley Kubrick's seminal science-fiction epic *2001: A Space Odyssey* was originally written by German composer Richard Strauss. Strauss called the piece "Also sprach Zarathustra," after the book of that name by philosopher Friedrich Nietzsche.

"*Secular millenarianism*," as defined by the American Encyclopedia of Religion: "*A belief that the end of the world is at hand, and that in its wake will appear a New World, inexhaustibly fertile, harmonious, sanctified, and just.*"

The millennial Expo 2000 in Hannover, Germany, will offer plenty of sustenance for the culture-hungry: Composer Heiner Goebbels has written an opening anthem for the festival; rock band the Scorpions will join the Berlin Philharmonic for an open-air concert; and director Peter Stein will stage a nineteen-hour rendition of *Faust.*

La-Z-Boy is manufacturing a line of office chairs called "Millennia." The chairs have "a very contemporary look," according to a La-Z-Boy executive. Could this be the future of comfort?

> *"**A**ll do live /
> in different periods,
> to themselves unknown."*
>
> —*Francis Dobbs,* Millennium,
> A Poem *(1787)*

By mid-1997, the Rainbow Room restaurant in Manhattan had already sold out two hundred seats for the night of December 31, 1999. Diners at the sixty-fifth-floor restaurant will pay a minimum of $1,000 each for the New Year's honor.

According to the Gregorian calendar, leap year normally occurs once every four years, but a "century year" is only considered a leap year when it is divisible by four hundred. Thanks to this rule, neither 1800 nor 1900 were leap years; the year 2000, however, *will* be a leap year.

Life in the year 2000—a prediction:

"*B*ecause everything in her home is waterproof, the housewife of 2000 can do her daily cleaning with a hose."

—Popular Mechanics, *1950*

To commemorate the millennium, a New Zealand organization called TimeVault 2000 is planning to build a huge pyramid-shaped time capsule—the "Millennium Vault"—filled with objects and memorabilia from the end of the twentieth century. The group hopes its vault will be opened in the year 3000.

San Francisco's BankAmerica has established a $30 million bonus pool to be shared by the six hundred computer experts debugging the bank's computers for the year 2000—provided the programmers stick with the company through the fateful date.

To acknowledge the millennium, the National Endowment for the Arts is planning to televise nationwide a series of "Millennium Minutes"—brief profiles of significant people and events of the last thousand years.

"Within a thousand years, we will break forever the bonds of gravity and soar freely among the stars. This Great Divide in the topography of time coincides with the dawn of the

Third Millennium. The coming Millennium is the Age of Aquarius—prelude to the endless emerald epoch of Life's galactic empire."

—*Marshall T. Savage*, The Millennial Project: Colonizing the Galaxy in 8 Easy Steps *(1997)*

> "**A**ny name sounds cool when you add '2000' to it."
>
> —*filmmaker Ellie Lee, 1995*

"Yes, golf, that pastime of ill-dressed fogies and Pecksniffian elitists, is turning a hip and trendy corner as the millennium approaches."

—Los Angeles Times, *July 23, 1996*

Environmentalists in Paris will honor
the millennium by building a two
hundred-meter-tall wooden "Earth
Tower." Sponsored by UNESCO, their
tower will be constructed with wood
from five different continents, and
should be completed by the
end of 1999.

*"**V**irtually none of your appliances should have a problem. And even if a VCR should fail, what's the big deal? Most VCRs don't last that long anyway."*

—Lindsey Vereen, editor of Embedded Systems Programming *magazine, addressing fears about the Y2K problem in the home*

Medieval Burgundian monk Radulphus Glaber wrote that "an enormous dragon, coming out of the North and reaching the South, throwing off sparks," was seen flying over Europe three years before the end of the first millennium A.D.

The Ritz hotel in London received so many inquiries about reservations for the night of December 31, 1999, that it chose to not take any at all. Instead, the hotel intends to assign the rooms by lottery.

Many astronomers, frustrated by the confusing Gregorian calendar, instead use the "Julian day calendar," conceived by Joseph Justus Scaliger in 1583. That system starts from a zero point in 4713 B.C. and measures no weeks, months, or years—only an endless series of uniquely numbered days.

As part of its New Millennium Program, NASA hopes to blast into the next century with a series of frequent, but inexpensive, unmanned space missions. The planned "armadas" of robot craft will serve as a "virtual human presence" throughout the universe.

"As the most recent apocalyptic event, Heaven's Gate joins a growing list of millennial outbreaks which are only now receiving the attention they deserve. Included among these

incidents are Jonestown, Ruby Ridge,
Waco, Aum Shinri Kyo, and
The Solar Temple."

—Aaron M. Katz, "Heaven's Gate: A Harbinger Of
Things To Come?" (1997)

Some experts advise that consumers demand written statements from credit card issuers, mortgage holders, and insurance companies attesting that they are "year 2000 compliant." Holding such a letter might allow individuals to join in class-action lawsuits if the feared "computer crisis" does occur in January 2000.

*"**B**y now it's a cliché to note that since historical changes don't obey the calendar, the year 2000 is bound to be historically neutral."*

—*Paul O'Donnell*, Washington Post *(1997)*

In August of 1997, organizers of New York's Times Square 2000 party announced that the first corporate sponsor of the event would be Korbel Champagne.

Gaining momentum: In January of 1997, there were 50,000 sites on the World Wide Web containing the phrase "year 2000." By January of 1998, that number had swelled to more than 285,000—an increase of 570 percent.

The term *mal du siècle*—French for "century sickness"—was coined by the Vicomte François René de Chateaubriand to describe the uncomfortable social and political climate as the eighteenth century drew to a close.

A select group of New Year's revelers in St. Petersburg, Russia, plan to say a glamorous farewell to the 1900s with a "Tsar's New Year's Eve Ball."

To prepare the National Airspace System for the Y2K rollover, computer programmers working for the Federal Aviation Administration are faced with the task of de-bugging twenty-two million lines of software code on 297 interrelated computer systems.

The "Millennium Dome" in Greenwich, England, will contain eleven huge, separate stages for events.

"Catholic, Lutheran, Methodist, and other clergy still feel a little uneasy speaking to millennial questions that lie outside their ordinary training. But this stuff *is so permeating popular culture and new religious movements, they will have to. Their congregations are demanding it."*

—*Michael Barkun,* author of several books on millennial issues

Ruth S. Freitag of the Library of
Congress has compiled a 232-source
bibliography on the subject of when,
properly speaking, centuries roll over.
Almost all of her sources—and the library
itself—agree that the twentieth century
will not end until
December 31, 2000.

> *"**I** sense that I am alive at a time of important change, and I feel a responsibility to make sure that the change comes out well. I plant my acorns knowing that I will never live to harvest the oaks."*

—Danny Hillis, *"The Millennium Clock,"*
Wired *on-line*

The National Science Foundation will celebrate its fiftieth anniversary in the year 2000, and plans to launch a national campaign that year to emphasize the importance of science, engineering, and mathematics.

Adding insult to injury: In addition to the much talked-about Y2K problem, computer experts announced in 1998 that they had discovered another glitch for the millennium. Because A.D. 2000 is a rare "century leap year"—the first in four hundred years—many older software programs may completely skip a day at the end of February that year.

The Swedish government, proud of its commitment to high technology, claims that by the year 2000, 85 percent of Swedes will have e-mail access.

Some apocalyptic Christian groups believe that the world will end on the millennium with a "cosmic battle" on Israel's Plain of Jezreel. In an effort to accommodate onlookers to the event, the Israeli National Park Authority is busily improving tourist accommodations in the area.

When Peter Kalikow opened a hotel in lower Manhattan, he named it "The Millenium"—misspelling the word with only one "n." Kalikow later told the *Wall Street Journal* that "it looked lousy with two n's."

> "*If there is one point on which both secular forecasters and inspired mystics agree, it is that during the brief two and a half decades separating us from the year 2000, the present world order will undergo a total change.*"

—*Omar V. Garrison*, Encyclopedia of Prophecy *(1978)*

For millennial celebrants with New Age leanings, Deja Vu/Spiritual Adventure Tours of Berkeley, California, is offering a New Year's trip to the Amazonian rain forest. According to the company's spokesperson, "We'll communicate with the energy of the universe. Plus, it's a party, of course."

Heeding the pope's call to prepare for the "Great Jubilee 2000," a Catholic shrine in Belleville, Illinois, is installing on its grounds a sculpture entitled *Flamma, MMM.* The sculpture—a twisted stainless steel spire—is said to resemble a candle flame; its title means "Flame 3000" in Latin.

*"**S**ince our century bears the same relation to the next millennium as the nineties bear to a new century, that tenseness characteristic of the experience of any fin de siècle has already been ascribed to the 1900s in their entirety."*

—*Hillel Schwartz*, Century's End

Preparing for a huge onslaught of visitors during the Catholic "Great Jubilee 2000," the city of Rome has "reclaimed" a number of flophouses and brothels around its central train station. Pilgrims can now rest safely, authorities insist.

The first total solar eclipse of the next millennium will occur on June 21, 2001, darkening a portion of Africa and the island of Madagascar.

The Church of England has created a "millennium team" to keep its image up-to-date and help ease its transition into the future.

"*Clearly, we have now entered the 'hot zone' of millennial time—the optimum span of one to four years distance for apocalyptic predictions, in which hopes and expectations are*

raised to a fever pitch and believers sustain a maximum level of missionary and preparatory activity."

—*Stephen D. O'Leary, "Heaven's Gate and the Culture of Popular Millennialism" (1997)*

In the summer of 2000, the Place de la Concorde in Paris will be turned into a huge sundial. The landmark Egyptian obelisk in the center of the Place will serve as the sundial's needle, with the dial itself laid out on the ground below.

> *"We would be a paltry generation if, at this crucial juncture in our global civilization, with all the crises we face, we met the passing of a millennium with a skeptical shrug and a nose to the grindstone."*

—*from the Center for Millennial Studies web site*

Television network ABC has asked ten of America's most prominent playwrights—including David Mamet, Steve Martin, Neil Simon, and Wendy Wasserstein—to pen screenplays about "what the year 2000 means." The teleplays will run during the sweeps of November 1999.

CCC

"To be fin de siècle *is to be no longer responsible; it is to resign oneself in a nearly fatal fashion to the influence of the times and environs. . . . It is to languish with one's century, to decay along with it."*

—anonymous French journalist, 1886

In A.D. 993, a violent volcanic eruption shook Italy's Mount Vesuvius. According to some historians, Europe's fervently religious populace took the event to be a sinister omen of the approaching second millennium.

Some Hindus are predicting an apocalypse of their own—set to take place at the end of the age Kali (A.D. 2003 by the Christian calendar).

A group of nautical history buffs in England intend to celebrate the millennium by reenacting one of the most celebrated sea voyages in history. The organizers of Mayflower 2000 are building a replica of the ship that

brought the pilgrim fathers to America, and hope to sail their vessel from Plymouth, England to Massachusetts in time for the millennial turnover.

> "**A**ll great 'dates' effect the period before and after, when apocalyptic hopefuls either jump the gun or 'redate' after prophecy fails."

—*Richard Landes*, Apocalyptic Expectations around the Year 1000

In preparation for New Year's Eve 1999, French champagne maker Perrier-Jouet will offer for sale two thousand jeroboams—bottles four times the standard size—filled with its 1995 vintage. The suggested retail price will be $2,000 per bottle.

They live to shop: Since 1997, a forty-member team of "Y2K investigators" has been traveling the globe equipped with American Express "test cards" bearing post-2000 expiration dates. Numerous credit validation systems worldwide have balked at the cards, AmEx reports.

*"**T**he people rushing toward the millennium with their fingers on the keyboards of the Information Age could become one of the most powerful political forces in history. . . . No other social group is as poised to dominate culture and politics in the twenty-first century."*

—Jon Katz, Wired *magazine*

"**I** don't know if I'll be in Egypt sitting under a pyramid or onstage, but that's a very spiritual time. My basic things for the year 2000 are to stay positive, centered, focused, and to leave that cocaine alone."

—musician Rick James

Both Japan and Detroit are hoping the year 2000 will help boost car sales. Mazda is offering a model called the Millennia; Chrysler is pushing a model called the Millennium.

"There is a general feeling that something spectacular ought to happen in the year 2000 or perhaps the summer of 1999."

—*Mike Dash,*
publisher of The Fortean Times

"**I**f it's only about the birth of Christ, fair enough—we wish our Christian brothers well. But if it is about Britain in the year 2000, Islam should have a place in the dome."

—*Bashir Abrahim-Khan, spokesman for the golden mosque in Regent's Park, London, on Muslim representation at the "Millennium Dome"*

Although England's Royal Greenwich Observatory maintains that the next millennium begins in year 2001—*not* 2000—it is nevertheless licensing out its "Greenwich Meridian 2000" logo to corporate sponsors. Admits a spokesperson: "Our purpose is to draw sponsors. Frankly, the year 2000 appeals to more people."

"As the year 2000 thunders in with that portentous plop, that mildly derisory anti-climax which is the fated doom of the purely chronogrammatical *jour de fête, the chances are three to one or thereabouts that in southern England it will be raining."*

—New York Times Magazine, *December 26, 1954*

*"**O**ne begins to get a feeling that by the time the year 2000 rolls around, we're all going to be sick and tired of hearing about it."*

—*C.W. Gusewelle,* Kansas City Star

While the world was busy welcoming the arrival of the twentieth century on December 31, 1900, a forceful gale on England's Salisbury Plain blew over one of the ancient monumental stones at Stonehenge.

The year 2000 will also mark the two hundredth anniversary of the founding of the Library of Congress.

"*If we have to spend a million to make it the party of a lifetime, we will.*"

—David Hosea, co-developer of the planned "Millennium Tower" in Newport, Kentucky, describing his hopes for December 31, 1999

"So much whirls in our heads as we barrel toward 2000, stuff we Americans are not good at, like history, and stuff we practice all too well, like weirdthink: UFO believers saying that this time the *aliens really, really mean it; conspiracy believers saying that at last the dark forces are really, really gonna let us have it."*

—*Patt Morrison,*
Los Angeles Times Magazine *(1997)*

"**N**ow we are on the verge of a new century, and what country's name will it bear? I say it will be another American century."

—*George Bush, in his speech accepting the Republican presidential nomination, 1988*

Life in the year 2000—a prediction:

"Whales will be kept in captivity, bred and herded like cattle."

—New York Times Magazine, *1954*

> ## "The impact of Christian civilization on Western civilization will be central to the project."

—Peter Mandelson, British minister in charge of the millennial celebration in Greenwich, referring to festivities at the "Millennium Dome"

> "*Even very secular people are likely to experience a millennial moment or two in the next few years.*"
>
> —*John Yemma*, Boston Globe, *1997*

La Fura dels Baus, a performance group from Spain's Catalonia region, plan to celebrate the millennium by staging a worldwide twenty-four-act piece entitled "Big Opera Mundi." Each act will take place in a different time zone at precisely midnight, December 31, 1999, and will be broadcast on the World Wide Web.

To honor the advent of the twentieth century, financier Leopold Rothschild sent a pair of pheasants to every omnibus driver in London on December 31, 1900.

"The millennium myth teaches that
we are living in the final days
of human history; it perpetuates the
idea that the present generation is in
some way 'chosen,' having some role

to play in either witnessing or participating in the culmination of the final days prophesied in various written sources."

—Aaron M. Katz, *"Heaven's Gate: A Harbinger Of Things To Come?" (1997)*

One plan discussed for the Times Square celebration of New Year's Eve 1999—but rejected by festival organizers—was to have a "space saucer" land in Times Square and fake an alien abduction.

"**N**o one is going to be able to trademark the new millennium."

—*Jim Andrews, vice president of information service company IEG*

*"**T**here's a lot of talk even in the mainstream about stockpiling food, water, ammunition—laying away enough stuff to see you through a year or two of super hard times."*

—*Ted Daniels, publisher of* The Millennial Prophecy Report, *on the subject of millennial preparations*

By late 1997, Manhattan's sixty-fifth-floor Rainbow Room Restaurant—though already fully booked for New Year's Eve, 1999—had added an additional nine hundred names to a waiting list for reservations. Plenty of seating for December 31, 2000, was still available, however.

*"**U**ndoubtedly, the turning of the millennium will be one of the largest commercial events of our lifetime."*

—*Millennium Society cochairperson
Cathleen Magennis Wyatt*

Vintners in New Zealand—just west of the international date line—boast that their grapes will be the first in the world to bask in the sunshine of the next millennium. Wine shoppers can look forward to a heavily marketed New Zealand vintage for the year 2000.

A San Diego memorabilia company called "Class of 2000" has this stern message for anyone thinking of appropriating its name: "Please don't mess with our registered trademark or you could end up behind bars beyond the year 2000."

> *"**A**lthough often depicted as a fringe phenomenon, millenarianism is extremely pervasive."*
>
> —Daniel Wojcik, University of Oregon

For the big celebration of December 31, 1999, rooms at London's Savoy hotel have been sold out since 1990.

For pious Jews, the advent of the third millennium A.D. may have no meaning. But some rabbis maintain that 240 years later—year 6000 by the Jewish calendar—the Messiah will arrive.

"**A**s we approach the millennium, we are acutely aware of how many people are beginning their articles with the phrase 'as we approach the millennium.'"

—*Charles Gordon,* MacLean's *magazine*

For the children who completed kindergarten in 1988, teachers across America held particularly festive "graduation" ceremonies—because those same children would later constitute the high school "Class of 2000."

*"**N**o airplane will fall out of the sky or go off course because of the year 2000 problem, and no elevator is going to crash to the ground. But there will be even wilder rumors as the time nears."*

—Norman Kurland, *Computer Professionals for Social Responsibility*

An early king of Poland, Boleslav the Brave, converted to Christianity in A.D. 999. Some historians believe his conversion may have been prompted by a case of the millennial jitters—better to enter the year 1000 safe than sorry.

According to polls conducted in the mid-1990s by Saatchi & Saatchi Advertising, only 7 percent of consumers felt "pessimistic" about the impending millennium.

In 1989, the New Age College of Massage in Fort Dodge, Iowa, changed its name to the Millenium College of Massage. The new, misspelled name came to the school's owner, Angie Eldridge, in a late-night revelation: "Everybody tells me it's wrong, but that's the way it came in."

> "**A**s we get closer to the millennium, there is a greater and greater anxiety among the human race. . . . More and more people are looking for answers or a plan."
>
> —*Phillip Lucas, editor,* Nova Religio

One of the goals of NASA's New Millennium Program is to send "a basketball-sized spacecraft to rendezvous with a speeding comet."

"There have been lots of suicides on a small scale, and I don't think it's unlikely that we'll see more as the millennium nears."

—Marcia Rudin, head of the New York office of the American Family Foundation, a national cult research organization

"*The* millennium must be a Christian celebration."

—Richard Harris, Anglican Bishop of Oxford, who opposes the commercialization of the event

"I have seen talk shows, read articles and heard reports of some of the antics of the Class of 2000, and instead of feeling proud, I feel ashamed. Thanks to the few teenage exhibitionists who go on trashy TV talk shows that

shamelessly exploit ignorant people, we are being remembered not as the future of the millennium, but as the screw-ups who will some day govern our world."

—letter to Ann Landers from M.R., Albany, New York, a member of the class of 2000

CCCLI

Boro Machine Co. of Riegelsville, Pennsylvania, is offering a golf putter called the Millennium. The company states that the putter's revolutionary design results from "the passion of a man who has spent a lifetime trying to perfect his golf game."

In 1912, Americans flocked to theaters to see a silent movie called *In the Year 2000*. What audiences were so excited about, no one knows. The film has vanished; not a single print remains.

"**W**e invite all users of the Internet to join us in drinking a toast to the Queen at 1.00pm/ 13.00hrs (local time) on the first day of the millennium to wish her good health, our way of saying 'thanks ma'am' for being a superb monarch."

—from the Web site of Ivor Spencer, founder of England's "Guild of Professional Toastmasters"

In order to capitalize on their "first light of the millennium" prominence, a group of twelve Pacific island nations—including Fiji, Kiribati, Tonga, and the Cook Islands—formed a marketing alliance called the "Millennium Consortium" in mid-1997.

America's love affair with television will be a half-century old in the year 2000. TV hit it big in 1950—nearly fifty million sets were introduced to American homes that year.

On a web site hosted by Chicago's Billennium Organizing Committee, people with high-flying hopes can electronically post their New Year's resolutions for the millennium. The resolutions will be uploaded to a satellite scheduled to launch into space on the year 2000.

> *"**I** would make sure I have at least a one-year paper trail on any significant transactions—mortgages, stocks, insurance—just in case something happens to electronic records at those places."*

—Michael Higgins, president of a Maryland computer consulting firm, on preparing for the year 2000 computer problem

"So here we are at the end of the millennium, more or less masters of the material universe. We have flying machines, we have cordless phones, we have no-stick frying pans. Ho hum. What's next?"

—*Rob Riddell,* Wired *magazine*

Investment banker John Veronis and his wife, Lauren, paid $2 million to reserve the Grand Ballroom of New York's Plaza Hotel for the evening of December 31, 1999.

The first child born on January 1, 2000, will have been conceived on or about April Fools' Day, 1999.

To help clarify the end-of-the-century (00–01) argument, French astronomer Jacques Cassini developed an alternate timeline in 1740. He proposed renaming 1 B.C. as the year zero, then setting back all dates B.C. by one year.

The result would not affect any years A.D., *but would cause centuries to begin decisively in "00" years. (Sadly, the system was never widely accepted.)*

In Edwin A. Abbott's bizarre metaphorical novel *Flatland*, first published in 1884, all the characters inhabit an alternate two-dimensional world. Until New Year's Eve, 1999, that is—when the book's protagonist, A. Square, has a revelation that allows him to perceive the world in three dimensions. Prophetic?

*"**M**y plan for the millennium is to save rock-and-roll from my senseless and unimaginative peers, and to look good while doing so."*

—musician Marilyn Manson

Mine? I'm null.
(anagram for "millennium")

In December 1997, Nevada became the first state to pass legislation categorizing Y2K data disasters as "acts of God"— protecting the state from lawsuits that may potentially be brought against it by residents in the year 2000.

CCCLXVII

*"**B**ooks on the twentieth or twenty-first century are getting to be so numerous that the whole subject will soon be a deadly bore."*

—The Literary World, *1890*